HERBERT S. ZIM

OWLS

Newly Revised Edition
illustrated by James Gordon Irving
and René Martin

William Morrow and Company
New York 1977

Thanks are due to A. L. Nelson, Patuxent Research Refuge, for critical help with the original manuscript and to Carol McClintock for aid in the revision.

Metric measure, now used the world over, is used in this book. Lengths and distances are based on the meter (m); 100 centimeters (cm) make one meter and 1000 meters make one kilometer (km). Weights are in kilograms (kg); 1000 grams (g) make one kilogram (kg).

A meter is just under 40 inches; a kilometer is 0.6 miles. A kilogram equals 2.2 pounds.

Library of Congress Cataloging in Publication Data

Zim, Herbert Spencer (date)
  Owls.

  SUMMARY: Introduces the owl, whose silent flight enables it to capture many careless rodents.
  1. Owls—Juvenile literature. [1. Owls] I. Irving, James Gordon. II. Martin, René, fl. 1965- III. Title.
QL696.S8Z5 1977   598.9'7   76-52927
ISBN 0-688-32109-7 lib. bdg.

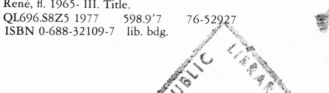

GREAT
HORNED
OWL

Owls are easy to recognize, for they look like nothing but owls. They are birds admirably adapted for hunting at night. Their odd appearance has come about mainly from their night feeding. Rings of short, flattened feathers form a facial disc around the owl's large, staring eyes. The beak hooks sharply down and looks a bit like a nose. Some owls have tufts of feathers on their heads that stick out like ears, and soft, fluffy feathers make them look larger than they really are.

The owl's humanlike head and its weird calls led people, long ago, to believe that owls were spirits or had magic powers. Their hooting was taken as a sign that someone would soon die. So owls were feared or sometimes worshiped. Athena, the Greek goddess of wisdom, favored the owl, so it also became a symbol of wisdom, though it is no wiser than any other bird.

Owls form a large group, or order, of birds, which is divided into two families. In the first are barn owls, which total 10 kinds, or species. In the second are all the rest of the owls, which come to about 123 species. Owls are found all over the world except in the Antarctic and on small distant islands. Some 20 species live in North America and about 15 in Europe.

The tiny elf owl is barely 15 centimeters long, and many others are only the size of a robin. But, in general, owls are large birds.

ELF OWL
15 cm

ROBIN
21 cm

THE GREAT GRAY OWL, averaging 75 cm long, is probably the longest owl. It has a well-formed facial disc.

The great gray owl, widespread in the north, may grow over five times as tall as the elf owl, with a wingspan of some one and a half meters. The snowy owl and the horned owls are large too. In the horned-owl group are the eagle owls of Africa, Europe, and Asia.

Owls live from the Arctic to the tropics. They are at home in the mountains and along the shores, in deep forests, fields, swamps, and deserts. Most prefer wild regions, but forest species are more common near the forest edge, where they are close to more open feeding areas. The wild areas of the earth are constantly shrinking and so are the areas where most owls can live and hunt.

Some owls, like the barn and screech owls, get along quite well living close to man. Once they nested on cliffs, ledges, and in hollow trees. Now some prefer steeples, lofts, and barns. They live and nest near houses, even in cities and their suburbs.

Nevertheless, owls were around long before men. Scientists have studied their fossil remains and pieced together their evolution.

Buried in rocks about 150 million years old are bones of the earliest known birds. During the next hundred million years, more and more kinds of birds were preserved as fossils. Some kinds lived in the seas, others on land. But there were no owls until about 50 million years ago. Rocks of that age have yielded bones of an owllike bird.

In time, other kinds of birds appeared — gulls, pigeons, ducks, parrots, hawks, and owls more like those of today. In rocks about 36 million years old were fossil bones of horned and long-eared owls. During the next 10 million years, barn owls and spotted owls appeared.

Fossils of birds are very rare. So it is not surprising that knowledge of early owls is limited. One expert points out that seed

Millions of Years Ago	HISTORY OF OWLS OVER MILLIONS OF YEARS
1	Owls spread widely as the Ice Age comes to an end.
10 20 30 40	Owls continue to develop all through this period. Some are very much like owls of today. About 75 kinds have been identified from fossil bones.
50	first fossil ancestors of owls
100	several kinds of fossil seabirds
150	Archaeopteryx, the earliest toothed bird
200	several kinds of flying reptiles

plants spread widely about 25 million years ago. With such plentiful food, rodents may have increased and spread also. And owls, in turn, would benefit from an abundant food supply of rodents.

At any rate, fossil finds show that during the last million years or so owls spread worldwide and developed into the many kinds known today. Thus, they have become a common and successful group of predatory birds.

Most present-day owls are gray or brown with broken patterns of lighter and darker feathers. This mottled, spotted, and striped coloring makes owls almost invisible against the bark or on the branches of trees, where they usually perch by day. The changing pattern of light and shadow amid the trees also helps keep owls concealed. The near-white snowy owl is camouflaged in its natural surroundings too. It can hardly be seen against the snow or on sand dunes along the shore. The only owls with strongly marked plumage are the spectacled owl and a few others, all in South America.

Owls are birds of the night, flying, hunting, and feeding at dusk or later. When it is so dark you can scarcely see, owls can see very well. But some owls also hunt by day. In the Arctic, where the snowy owl lives, there is no darkness in the summer. So hunting must be done while the sun is above the horizon.

The smallish hawk owl of northern Canada and similar sub-Arctic areas of Europe also feeds by day. So does the short-eared owl, an open-country bird. Owls can see by day, but at night they see much, much better.

SHORT-EARED OWL

Owls that hunt by day usually prefer more open areas. They are less owllike than night-flying owls.

SNOWY OWL

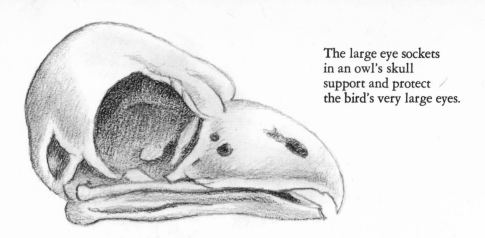

The large eye sockets in an owl's skull support and protect the bird's very large eyes.

An owl's eyes are tremendous. Those of a large owl are about as big as a person's. Considering the bird's size, these eyes are large indeed. An owl's eyes take up more space in the skull than the brain itself. The eyes of backboned animals are all built on the same general plan. Those of an owl are quite like human eyes. Some parts of its eyes are better developed, some not as well.

Owl's eyes look large not only because they are but because of their bright color. A few owls have brown or dark eyes. All the rest are yellow or yellowish.

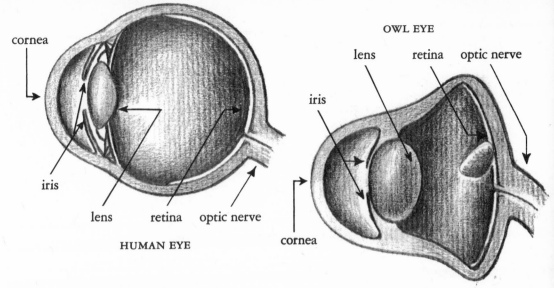

cornea

iris

lens   retina   optic nerve

HUMAN EYE

OWL EYE

lens   retina   optic nerve

iris

cornea

Near the front of the eye is a thin tissue, the iris, which gives the eye its color. At the center of the iris is a hole, the pupil, through which light enters the eye. Tiny muscles attached to the iris can pull it back, making the pupils larger. Other muscles do the opposite and make the pupil smaller. In strong sunlight the pupil of the owl's eye becomes very small, and the bright yellow iris is easily seen. As the light becomes dimmer with evening, the pupil becomes larger and larger,

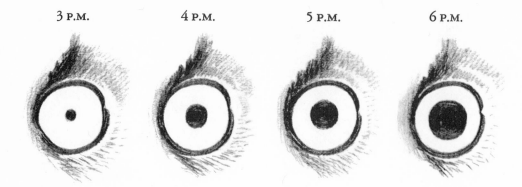

3 P.M.   4 P.M.   5 P.M.   6 P.M.

As daylight fades in the afternoon the size of the pupil increases.

and less of the iris shows. When the pupil is wide open at night, the iris is only a thin yellow or brown ring.

This ability of the eye to adapt to changing light is common among many animals.

LONG-EARED OWL

Since the distance between a pair of eyes is small, both receive the same amount of light and the size of the pupil in both eyes is the same. But an owl's eyes seem to act independently. Owls have been observed, and even photographed, with the pupil of one eye much larger than that of the other.

About sixteen times as much light enters the human eye when the pupil is fully open as when the pupil is at its smallest size. At least this much difference, possibly more, is true of owls.

LONG-EARED OWL

When the size of the pupil changes with light, both eyes usually change at the same rate. But owls are sometimes seen with one large and one small pupil.

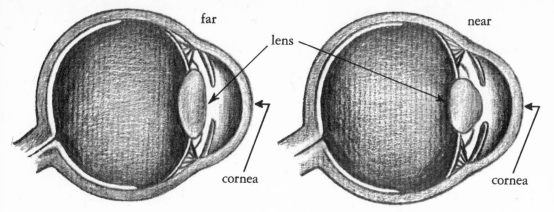

far   lens   near

cornea   cornea

IN THE HUMAN EYE, the lens changes and the cornea remains the same.

An owl's eye is designed for sharp, distant vision. It can spot a meadow mouse far below in the grass. But, though its eye makes some adjustment, the owl does not see nearby things as well.

In your eyes, small muscles automatically change the shape of the lens. They make it thicker when you read a book and stretch it thinner when you watch something at a distance. This adjustment for near and distant vision is called "accommodation."

In the owl's eye the lens does not change

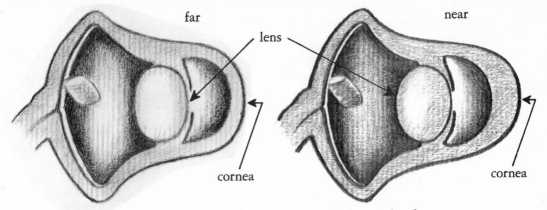

far lens near

cornea cornea

IN THE OWL'S EYE, the cornea changes and the lens remains the same.

much, but the outer transparent covering of the eye (the cornea) bulges or flattens somewhat. In effect, the owl has another set of lenses—a sort of built-in glasses.

Each human eye is protected by a pair of eyelids, which cover the eye automatically when something moves close or when there is some irritation. Owls have a pair of eyelids on each eye too. They also have a third, transparent eyelid that they can flip across their eye at will. It works automatically, like human eyelids when a person winks.

As a hunting owl strikes its prey, this transparent eyelid (called the "nictitating membrane") sweeps across the eye, protecting it from scratches, hair, or dirt. As it flicks across the eye, the membrane also helps keep the eye moist. Owls are also believed to use this third eyelid when the light is strong and when they are in flight.

The most important part of an owl's eyes, and of yours, is the delicate lining at the back of the eyeball. There, in the retina, are the cells that change the light waves which strike the eye into a message that gives the brain the image of what is seen.

This work is done by rod and cone cells, which make up the inner layer of the retina. Your eyes have both. The rod cells are sensitive to light of low intensity, the cone cells to bright light and to color. Owls have fewer cone cells and so they see only a world of grays. Yet the closely packed rod cells give them fine nighttime vision. The rod cells of the owl's eye are rich in a complex purple chemical that makes night vision possible. The eyes of owls that fly by day differ somewhat from those of owls that fly by night.

An owl's eyes are set for forward vision.

HORNED OWL   SPOTTED OWL

Another important thing about an owl's eyes is their position. Many birds have eyes on the sides of their head, almost as far back as your ears. Each eye can see on its side, but neither can see straight ahead. However, the eyes of owls and some other birds are in the front of the head. Both eyes see forward, and this overlapping view helps an owl judge the size, distance, and speed of its prey.

You turn your head or move your eyes when you want to see something to the right or left. An owl cannot move its eyes, but it turns its head easily. This movement looks odd, because an owl does not seem to have any neck. But it does, and it works better than yours. You have only seven neck bones, and the owl has fourteen. At each joint between bones, some movement is possible. So with more neck bones, the owl has more neck movement. It can turn its head much farther than you can; so much that it seems to look straight backward.

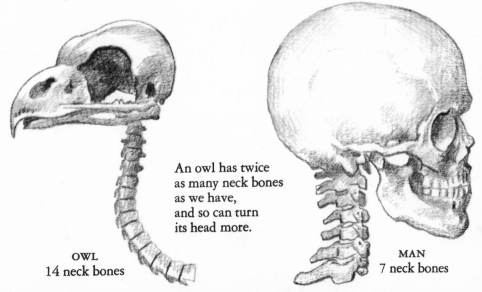

An owl has twice as many neck bones as we have, and so can turn its head more.

OWL
14 neck bones

MAN
7 neck bones

An owl can turn its head three quarters of the way around, or 270 degrees. All the way around is 360 degrees. A person can turn his or her head about 180 degrees — halfway around. Other animals can turn their head about as much as people can. Few equal the owl in this ability.

An owl will turn its head slowly till it is almost straight back. Then it may snap its head forward so fast that the movement is hard to follow. Once people thought the owl's head went completely around. They believed that if you walked around and around an owl, it would keep twisting its head until it would wring its own neck.

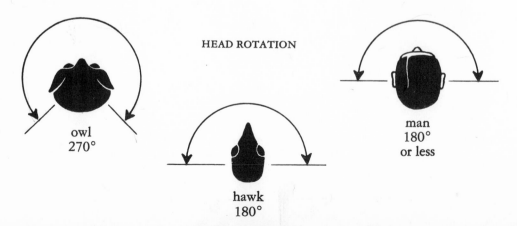

HEAD ROTATION

owl
270°

hawk
180°

man
180°
or less

The owl's fine sight is matched by its keen hearing. Birds have small, round earholes on the sides of their head. They do not have external ears like dogs or cats or people. Owls' ears have a long slit opening, with a flap of skin alongside. These flaps can be moved. But they are not seen, as they are covered by the feathers of the facial disc. Some owls have tufts or feathers on their heads that are called ears, but they have nothing at all to do with hearing.

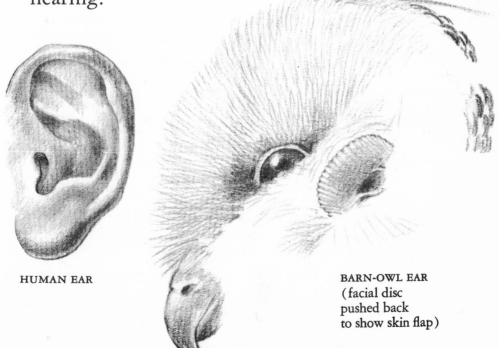

HUMAN EAR

BARN-OWL EAR
(facial disc
pushed back
to show skin flap)

The saucer-shaped spread of feathers that makes up the owl's face is believed to act like a sound reflector. It may amplify or build up the sound before it is picked up by the owl's ear slits.

As a result, owls can hear sounds much fainter than any you can pick up with your ears. They can also hear such high-pitched sounds as the squeal of a small rodent or the rustle of dry leaves. Hearing and responding instantly to such sounds leads the hunting owl to its prey.

FACIAL DISCS

barred owl

great
gray owl

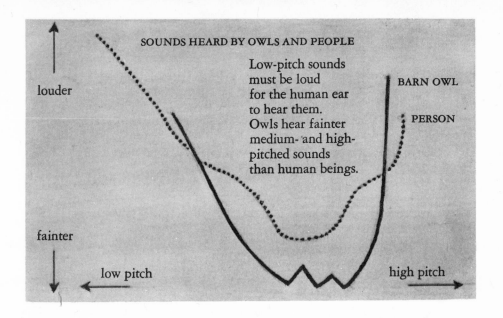

SOUNDS HEARD BY OWLS AND PEOPLE

Low-pitch sounds must be loud for the human ear to hear them. Owls hear fainter medium- and high-pitched sounds than human beings.

louder

fainter

low pitch

high pitch

BARN OWL

PERSON

In a laboratory, measurements of an owl's hearing and a person's were plotted into curves that could be compared. An owl can hear many faint sounds that you cannot hear at all. They may be of low, medium, or high pitch. Most sounds are complex mixtures of vibrations. An owl will respond, even if it hears only a part of them. Compared to other birds, the barn owl was found to be the most sensitive to sound.

Experiments with a barn owl show how important its hearing is. A scientist used a sound-proof room that could be totally darkened. He photographed the owl in darkness with an infrared camera and had sensitive instruments to measure sound.

A mouse ran across a foam-rubber floor, dragging a crumpled paper attached to its tail by a string. The mouse made very little noise, and the rustle of the paper was louder. In the darkness, the owl dived for the paper, not for the mouse.

When the mouse made its usual faint noises without the paper, the owl hit it 13 out of 17 times. When one of its ears was plugged shut, the owl missed the mouse by more than 30 centimeters.

As an owl flies, both its eyes and ears

point forward and tilt down toward the ground. No animal below has much chance of escaping unseen or unheard. The slightest movement or sound alerts the owl, which quickly and quietly gets into position to swoop down on its prey.

When other birds fly by, you can hear the swish and whirr of their beating wings if you are close enough. You cannot hear the wings of owls, however. Their flight is completely silent.

down feather

flight feather with comb or fringe

Young owls are covered with down, fine soft feathers that keep them warm but that are no use in flying. As the birds grow, they shed their down and gradually grow adult plumage. Much of this plumage is still soft feathers that preserve body heat and stream-line the bird. The wing feathers for flying, however, are quite different.

These flight feathers are usually long, narrow, firm, and stiff. They move the bird forward and provide the lift that takes it up. Flight feathers of owls are a bit shorter and more rounded than those of other birds of equal size.

Owl flight feathers have a soft fringe, or comb. This fringe was supposed to silence its flight. One curious scientist cut the fringe off each flight feather on a live owl. He checked the owl's flight. It was still silent. Now scientists are less sure why there is a fringe.

Some flightless birds, like the ostrich, have soft flight feathers. Some others, like penguins, have narrow flight feathers, too small to help in flying.

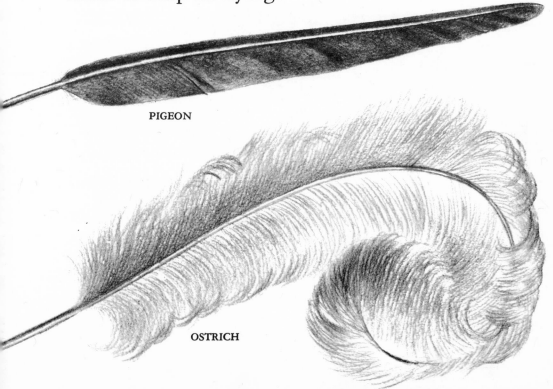

PIGEON

OSTRICH

Owls are not fast fliers. But they do not need speed, for they are concealed by darkness and by their silence. Owls are admirable birds of prey, though they lack the speed of falcons and the strength of eagles. They need a large supply of food. Large owls eat three or four mice or rats daily.

An owl locates its prey
by sight and sound,
plunging silently
with talons outstretched,
and does so
with unusual accuracy.

As an owl plunges down at its prey, its legs shoot forward. Each foot has four toes that end in curved, sharp, powerful talons. These built-in daggers are very much like those of hawks. But most hawks keep three toes forward and one back. Owls can move a second toe backward, thus spreading their talons for a better grip.

When an owl strikes, it seldom misses. Once it grabs hold, it seldom lets go. However, it usually kills its prey by biting it at the base of the skull. The talons are used mainly for holding. The legs and feet of most owls are covered with feathers. Those of most other birds are bare.

On the next pages are examples of some better known owls.

BARN OWL

perching

striking

BARN OWLS have heart-shaped facial discs, long wings, dark eyes, and bare feet. Some forms have a white breast, some orange. They and the closely related bay owls form a separate owl family, found mainly in temperate and warm regions. The common barn owl (illustrated) is about 40 centimeters tall. Barn owls have been brought to many small islands where rodents are a problem.

SCREECH OWLS may be 30 centimeters tall, but some in Asia are only half that. Many have a red and a gray color phase, and the number of each type varies in different places. All are mottled or barred in brown or darker colors and so are well hidden in trees. The kinds in Europe, Africa, and Asia (called scops owl) are both larger and smaller than American birds. Most screech owls nest in natural tree hollows or in deserted nest cavities made by woodpeckers and other birds.

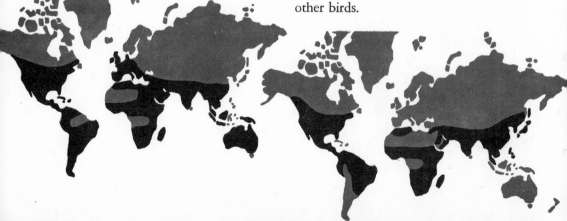

BURROWING OWLS are small (20 centimeters) and rather special. This owl lives and nests in burrows that it may dig or more often take from den-digging mammals like gophers and foxes. The brown-and-white spotted bird is easy to identify, and its colonies are easily found. Burrowing owls feed on insects and other small animals including birds, lizards, frogs, and toads.

PYGMY OWLS, including the owlets, are a group of about a dozen species. All are small—15 to 25 centimeters—but the least pygmy owl is reported as only 10 centimeters high. These tiny owls fly by day as well as night and have the odd habit of flicking their tail. Some have pleasant, whistling calls. All nest in natural or bird-made tree cavities. Pygmy owls take many kinds of insects for food. Some have a red and a gray color phase, like screech owls.

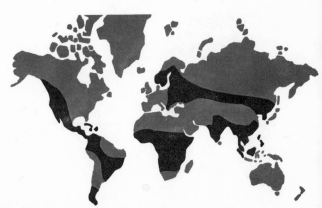

BARRED OWLS are typical of a group of common owls (11 species) with large heads, no eartufts, and a dark border around their facial discs. In this group are the short-eared owl and the great gray owl. The barred owl eats many rodents, but also feeds on song and game birds and quite a few kinds of fish. It has been observed to attack turtles—a difficult and perhaps dangerous feat.

SNOWY OWLS are birds of the far North, where they may nest while some snow is still on the ground. Since trees are very small or absent, the snowy owl uses any mound or small hill for nesting or for standing watch. One of the larger owls and also one of the most attractive, it is a wary bird and hard to approach. Eskimos used to raid the nests in spring and take the eggs for food.

SHORT-EARED OWLS belong to the group that also includes the long-eared owl. The short-eared is a more widespread species, marked by very small ear tufts and by light, fluffy markings. In some parts of its range the birds are darker. The short-eared owl is closely related to the African marsh owl. Both are about 35 centimeters high and are quite active by day.

SPOTTED OWLS are birds of western North America and members of the barred-owl group. This owl grows about 42 centimeters high. It is a fairly bulky bird, round-headed, and with feathered legs and feet. Its breast is light, spotted with brown. Two close relatives in South America are a bit smaller and more brightly colored.

SAW-WHET OWLS, a smaller species, rarely grow more than 19 centimeters long, but the female is a bit larger. The head (no ear tufts) seems unusually big for the body, and the eyes seem unusually large for the head. Together they create the impression of an odd, top-heavy bird.

The saw-whet owl ranges across North America. In the far North, however, it is replaced by the very similar, but slightly larger boreal owl, which also ranges across northern Europe and Asia. A close relative lives in Central America, and another in two distinct and separate areas in South America.

GREAT GRAY OWLS are a larger species. The male gets to a height of 75 centimeters, and the female reaches 85 centimeters. They have no ear tufts but do have a large facial disc. These northern birds prefer heavily wooded areas of fir and spruce. They feed mainly on forest rodents but may also take crows, grouse, and ptarmigans.

ELF OWLS, one of the smallest species, are sometimes only 12 centimeters in height. This owl's short tail makes it look even smaller. In weight, the elf owl averages about 25 grams—less than one ounce. A bird of warm areas, it is reputed to prefer the giant saguaro cactus for nesting, though it does nest in several other trees.

GREAT HORNED OWLS are known as the fiercest and most aggressive species. This owl dominates the western hemisphere, while the closely related eagle owls live in Europe, Asia, and Africa. Horned owls reach about 55 centimeters in height, and they have long ear tufts. Records show they eat a great variety of foods—many mammals, birds (including other owls), reptiles, amphibians, and fish.

PEL'S FISHING OWLS and several other kinds in Africa swoop down over the water and grab small fish at the surface. They nest in trees along streams and lakes and occasionally take other food. All have large heads and no ear tufts. Height is about 55 centimeters. Other species are smaller.

EAGLE OWLS are birds of Europe and Asia, but other eagle owls are found in Africa. All are in the same group as the great horned owl. The eagle owl averages some 70 centimeters in height, making it one of the largest owls. It and its relatives are forest birds, though some are adapted to desert areas. One, in central Africa, feeds only on insects.

SPECTACLED OWLS of South American rain forests have been known for nearly 400 years, but little has been written about this handsome and attractive species. The owl's striking brown, yellow, and white plumage and its large size (about 45 centimeters) set it apart. It seems to prefer being near water and is reported to eat crabs. Two similar species are also found in South America.

BARKING OWLS belong to a group called hawk owls, which consists of about a dozen species that live mainly in and near Australia. The barking owl is a brownish bird, mottled with white. It has a small facial disc, long, pointed wings, and typical yellow eyes. It is about 35 centimeters high. Most of the other hawk owls on South Pacific islands are a good deal smaller.

Owls are flesh eaters. Not a bit of plant food enters their diet. If the animal is small, like a beetle or a mouse, it is swallowed whole. To take care of this odd way of eating (somewhat like a snake's), the owl has a very special digestive system.

Powerful digestive juices dissolve all useful parts of the food. The skin, hair, bones, and teeth are worked into a tight, compact, oval pellet. This pellet takes about eight hours to form. Soon after, it is thrown up and the owl is rid of this undigested burden. None of the bones have been affected, and the pellet clearly shows what the owl has eaten.

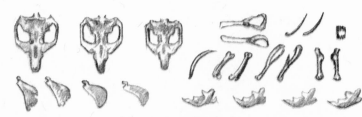

bones of meadow mice

BARN-OWL PELLET   feathers of an English sparrow

Scientists gather pellets and carefully take them apart. A three-year study showed that barn owls feed almost entirely on rodents. In the 2200 pellets examined, 6815 rodents were found. The barn owl's diet was 99 percent small mammals (90 percent mice) and 1 percent small birds.

By studying bones found in owl pellets, scientists have made discoveries about other animals in the area. Flying squirrels and two kinds of native mice were thus discovered in areas where they were not known before.

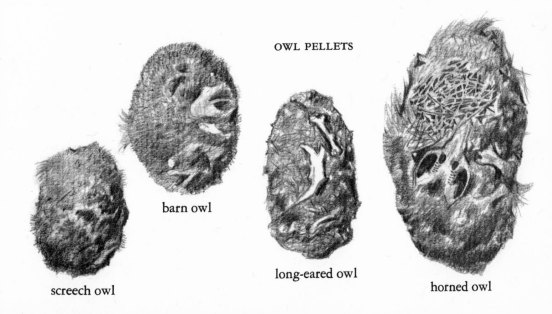

OWL PELLETS

barn owl

long-eared owl

horned owl

screech owl

**SNOWY-OWL INVASIONS
OF THE UNITED STATES**

1941

1945

1949

1953

1957

1960

1972
(Ontario)

1974
(British Columbia)

Food may also be the main reason why some owls move around. Most owls are permanent residents; they remain in the same area summer and winter. Only a few kinds, like the tiny elf owl and a small screech owl, are migrants, going south for the winter.

Owls set up a territory in which they hunt and raise their young. But the young, when out of their nest, also need land. They often wander hundreds of miles before they find and claim a territory of their own.

Snowy owls feed mainly on lemmings, which every few years go on a strange migration. About that often, snowy owls also move out, perhaps to follow their prey. They follow rivers and fly along shores, often going far to the south. One great "invasion" took place in 1942. Over 15,000 snowy owls came from Greenland and northern Canada into the Great Lakes region and New England.

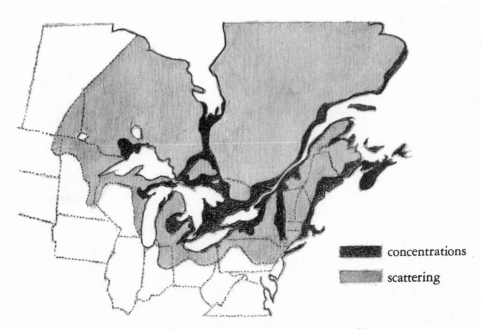

concentrations

scattering

INVASION OF SNOWY OWLS FROM CANADA IN 1942

In the fifty million years owls have been around, they have found many places to live. Owls nest from northern Greenland to the far southern tip of South America and on all of the seven continents, except Antarctica.

Screech owls range from the Sahara Desert in Africa to the high peaks of the South American Andes. Some live in evergreen timber, some in dry scrubland, some in island rain forests, and some amid desert rocks. The 31 kinds of screech owls are small and often appear in two color phases: gray and reddish.

GRAY
SCREECH
OWL

REDDISH
SCREECH
OWL

All owls that are widespread grow somewhat larger in cold parts of their range than in the warmer parts. This difference is true of barn owls, screech owls, and other species. In the horned-owl group, the north European owls are about 68 centimeters tall. The ones from Canada and northern United States grow up to about 50 centimeters. Birds from central and northern Africa are only 45 centimeters tall. Most of the small owls, like the pygmy and the elf owls, are birds of deserts or other warm regions.

THE COMMON BARN OWL,
together with similar species,
is found on six continents.
The smallest barn owls
are 27 to 28 centimeters tall,
the largest about 50 centimeters.

An observer usually cannot tell a male owl from a female on sight, If a pair is seen together, the smaller one is the male. He also calls with deeper notes. Only the snowy owls show other differences. The female is quite spotted; the male is nearly pure white.

Late in the winter the male owl starts to seek a mate. His calls echo through woods and fields. When a female responds, he brings her an offering of food. He fluffs out his feathers, makes displays and postures.

♀ female   male ♂

SCREECH OWLS

The courting male owl
brings food to the female.

male

female

SCREECH OWLS

This behavior attracts her attention and makes her willing to mate. The searching, calling, and courting is all done at night.

Most courting and mating
of owls take place at night.

SCREECH OWLS

After the male and female mate, they seek a nest. Sometimes it is a hole in a tree that flickers have abandoned. Screech owls may use a birdhouse or nest in a deserted house. Barn owls, too, prefer barns and other open buildings. Other owls sometimes use empty crow or hawk nests, hollow trees, or rocky ledges.

The burrowing owl makes a long underground burrow, which may twist and turn. At the end is its nest. It may also use the burrow of rabbits or prairie dogs. If the rabbits are still there, they may end up as food for the young owls.

The owl's nest may be almost nothing at all. At best it is poorly made of sticks or grass. It never shows the skill of an oriole or even of a robin.

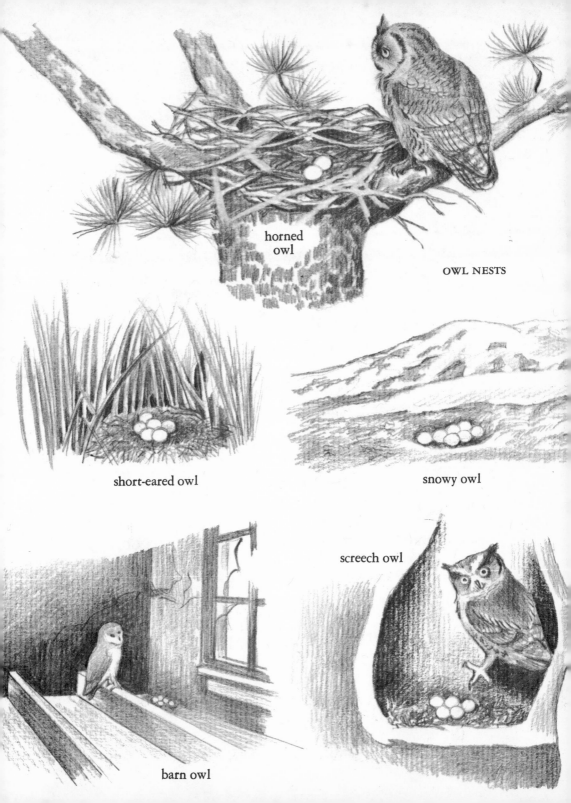

horned
owl

OWL NESTS

short-eared owl

snowy owl

screech owl

barn owl

In April, before warblers and thrushes have returned from the South, the female owls lay their eggs. Northern owls may lay while the snow is still on the ground. Because it is so early, the eggs sometimes freeze.

Owl eggs are white. Most are nearly round. The largest are almost as big as a hen's. The female owl may lay from two to thirteen eggs —usually four to seven. She often lays the eggs two to three days apart but begins to set from the very first day. Thus, when all the eggs are hatched, the oldest nestling is two or three weeks older than the youngest.

The female sets on the eggs to keep them warm. The male does his share by bringing food. Each night he will bring two to four rodents or other small animals to be sure his mate is well fed.

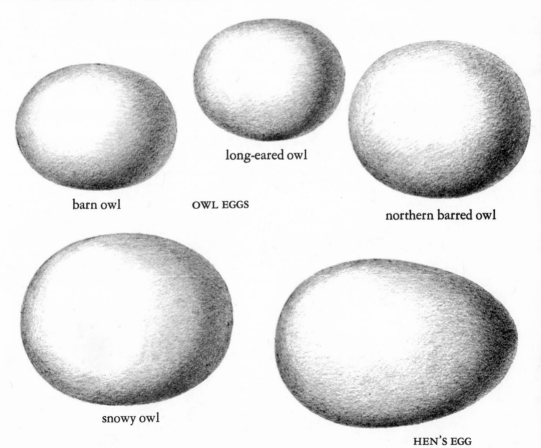

long-eared owl

barn owl   OWL EGGS

northern barred owl

snowy owl

HEN'S EGG

Owls' eggs hatch in 25 to 30 days more or less. The blind young work their way out of the shell and begin to clamor for food. At first the male brings it. Later the female helps

also. Insects may be fed whole, but larger prey is torn to bits by the mother.

Because the nestlings have hatched at different times, the first hatched is likely to be the largest and strongest. The last may be the weakest—the runt of the litter.

This difference becomes important if food is scarce. Then the larger birds become cannibals. While feeding, they may kill and eat the smaller, weaker nestlings. While this behavior may seem cruel, it enables a few strong birds to leave the nest instead of six or seven weak ones. The ones that live will have a better chance to survive. Even when food is plentiful, the older, stronger birds get the greater share. The others are not given as good a start in life.

The young remain in the nest for about six weeks, and every night the parents search far

SMALLEST SCREECH-OWL NESTLING

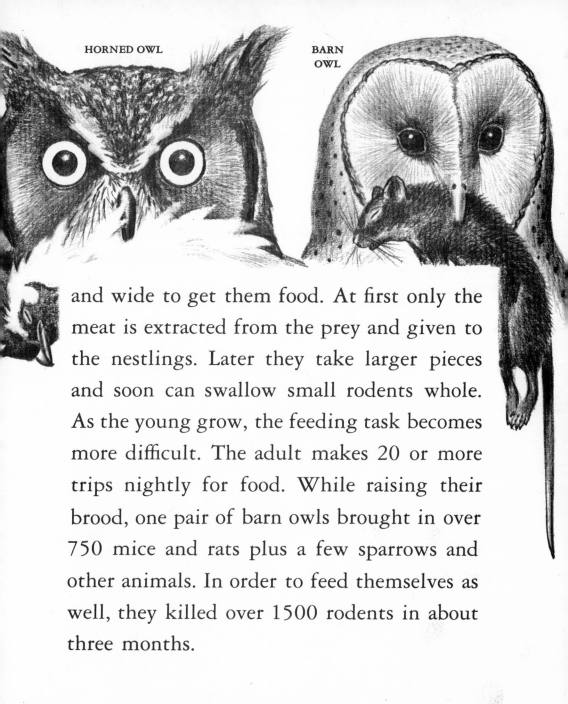

and wide to get them food. At first only the meat is extracted from the prey and given to the nestlings. Later they take larger pieces and soon can swallow small rodents whole. As the young grow, the feeding task becomes more difficult. The adult makes 20 or more trips nightly for food. While raising their brood, one pair of barn owls brought in over 750 mice and rats plus a few sparrows and other animals. In order to feed themselves as well, they killed over 1500 rodents in about three months.

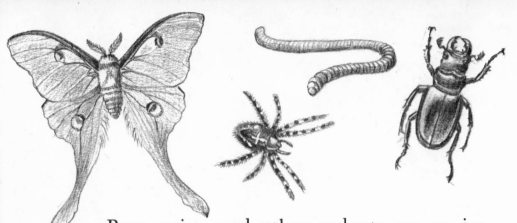

Rats, mice, and other rodents are an important part of the food of owls. In this way owls are helpful to farmers because of the damage rodents do to crops. But owls do not live for people alone. They have an important natural role as hunters. As such they eat a variety of foods.

The small owls feed on many kinds of insects, some of which they catch on the wing. They eat beetles, caterpillars, grasshoppers, moths, spiders, worms, frogs and lizards, mice, and small birds.

Larger owls feed on many kinds of mice and rats and also on squirrels (ground and

tree), prairie dogs, gophers, rabbits, hares, and skunks. Often they eat larger upland game birds, pigeons, and ducks.

Some species catch fish for food. They include the several fish owls, the bay owl, horned and eagle owls, and even the screech owl. In addition, snakes, crayfish, salamanders, lizards, bats, seabirds and shorebirds appear on the food list.

Feeding their nestlings and themselves keeps every pair of owls on the go. So much food is needed that even a change in the weather can affect the success of the parents. Experts watching nesting barn owls noted that for a few days after every rain, the parents brought back less food. Finally the reason became clear. Mice ran noiselessly over the wet soil, leaves, and grass. And without sounds to guide them, the parents had a harder job catching mice for their young.

DOWNY
BARN OWLS
ABOUT TWO WEEKS OLD

While the young are in or around the nest,
the parents go to great lengths to protect
them. If a human or animal intruder comes
close, the parents fluff up their feathers till
they look almost twice their size. They spread
their wings and snap their bills noisily. One
may pretend to be injured and, by limping or
fluttering, attempt to draw the intruder away
from the nest and the young.

If an intruder, such as an opossum or a raccoon, continues to approach, the adult owls do not hesitate to attack. Even if the intruder is a person fifty times as heavy as the owl, he will not be spared. The owl will fly above him, pause a second, and swoop down with talons outstretched. The talons are so sharp they can hurt and draw blood. Even the tiny elf owl has attacked bird watchers who have come too close to its saguaro-cactus nest.

BARN OWL THREATENING

SCREECH OWL
ATTACKING AN OBSERVER
AT ITS NEST HOLE

People and owls have not lived together well. For centuries owls, known as birds of bad omen, were killed whenever they were seen. Later owls were blamed for feeding on chickens. In fact, they rarely do so, though larger owls do take pigeons. Yet farmers shot all owls on sight. So did hunters, who claimed that owls destroyed quail and other game birds. Only in recent years has this kind of killing stopped.

Many birds have no love for owls. When one is found, they gather around to mob and attack it. Among these enemies are the hawks, which were also killed on sight by farmers. Knowing that hawks mobbed and attacked owls, farmers would catch an owl and tie it high in a tree. Or they would put up a stuffed owl. As soon as hawks spied the owl, they flew in to attack it. With this bait, farmers killed a large number of hawks.

Crows and jays are often seen mobbing an owl. Though the owl is a stronger bird, it does not fight back. The attackers may drive it from its perch. With all the noise and activity, the owl cannot rest, hunt, or feed. But when the sun sets and darkness comes, the owl is once again the silent, powerful master of the air.

INDEX
*indicates illustration